THE BEST OF BASS

Jam Trax

BLUES, R&B AND ROCK

by Ralph Agresta

The original just got better!
Full-band backup to 12 extended jams in authentic
blues, rhythm & blues and rock styles. Includes tips on
scales and techniques to use with each track.
In standard notation and tablature.

Cover photography supplied by Fender Frontline
with thanks to Del Breckenfeld and Adam St. James

This book Copyright © 1997 by Amsco Publications,
A Division of Music Sales Corporation, New York

All rights reserved. No part of this book may be
reproduced in any form or by any electronic or mechanical means,
including information storage and retrieval systems,
without permission in writing from the publisher.

Order No. AM 945307
US International Standard Book Number: 0.8256.1640.9
UK International Standard Book Number: 0.7119.6751.2

Exclusive Distributors:
Music Sales Corporation
257 Park Avenue South, New York, NY 10010 USA
Music Sales Limited
8/9 Frith Street, London W1V 5TZ England
Music Sales Pty. Limited
120 Rothschild Street, Rosebery, Sydney, NSW 2018, Australia

Printed in the United States of America by
Vicks Lithograph and Printing Corporation

 Music Sales America

DISTRIBUTED BY

HAL•LEONARD®
CORPORATION
7777 W. BLUEMOUND RD. P.O. BOX 13819 MILWAUKEE, WI 53213

Amsco Publications
New York/London/Sydney

CD Track Listing

1. Tuning
2. Twelve-Bar Blues in A
3. Twelve-Bar Rock 'n' Roll Blues in C
4. Twelve-Bar Very Slow Swing in G
5. Twelve-Bar Jazz Swing Feel in Bb
6. Knockin' On The Midnight Mustang
7. Why A Woman Loves A Man
8. Blues Boy
9. Funky Blue Street
10. Manic Inspiration
11. The Hindenburg Medley
12. Been Caught Sleeping
13. Pleasantly Lucid

Contents

Introduction

Hi! I'm Ralph Agresta. With the growing popularity of my *JamTrax* series, we've received tons of positive feedback and numerous requests to make *JamTrax* packages for other instruments. For this *Best of Blues, R&B, and Rock JamTrax for Bass*, I've enlisted the talents of John Abbey, who provided suggested scales and licks for each of these jams and condensed transcriptions of the parts that he played on the original "guitar" versions. These twelve tracks were selected from the *Blues JamTrax for Bass*, *R&B JamTrax for Bass*, and *Rock JamTrax for Bass* packages.

Everyone knows that the best way to learn or improve musical skills is to play with a live band, and now you can do just that in the privacy of your own room. Join either Chris Carroll, Phil Cimino, or Ernie Finamore (on drums), Phil Ricciardi (on keyboards), and me (on guitar and keyboards) for twelve blues, r&b, and rock jams. We'll play the drums, rhythm guitars, keyboards, and solos. You can play either the given bass parts (presented in both standard notation and tablature), or make up your own bass lines. Experienced players will enjoy using this CD to experiment with new ideas and techniques or for warming up before gigs. Beginners can practice playing without the pressure that often comes with performing in front of other people.

Inside this book you'll find, along with suggested scale patterns and riff samples, simple bass charts with chord symbols that will guide you through the structure of each jam.

Good luck, have fun, and, as always, I sincerely hope that you enjoy and learn from this CD.

Twelve-Bar Blues in A

This is a straight-ahead blues jam with a shuffle feel. The bassline is a repetitive phrase that uses the chord tones and scales tones called for by each of the three chords.

Pattern 1: A7, D7, and E7 arpeggios

Patterns 2, 3, 4, and 5: some variations

The fourth and eighth bars of the twelve-bar structure are the most common places to vary the bassline. Here are a couple of possibilities for each of these measures. Patterns 2 and 3 are for the fourth bar, while patterns 4 and 5 will work for bar eight.

pattern 2

pattern 3

pattern 4

pattern 5

Twelve-Bar Blues in A

Twelve-Bar Rock 'n' Roll Blues in C

This is another standard blues progression but with a straight feel. There's not much room to improvise over this track. Often a guitar will double a line like this with the bass, so you have to be careful about adding extra notes.

Here are some of the scale patterns that the bass line is derived from:

Pattern 1: C major pentatonic scale (one-octave)

Pattern 2: F major pentatonic scale (one-octave)

Pattern 3: G major pentatonic scale (one-octave)

Remember that these are not the only positions that these scales can be played in. This list represents only one set of possibilities.

Twelve-Bar Rock 'n' Roll Blues in C

Think of Little Richard's "Lucille" or the Beatles version of Larry William's
"Dizzy Miss Lizzy" when you play this track.

Medium straight-eighth feel

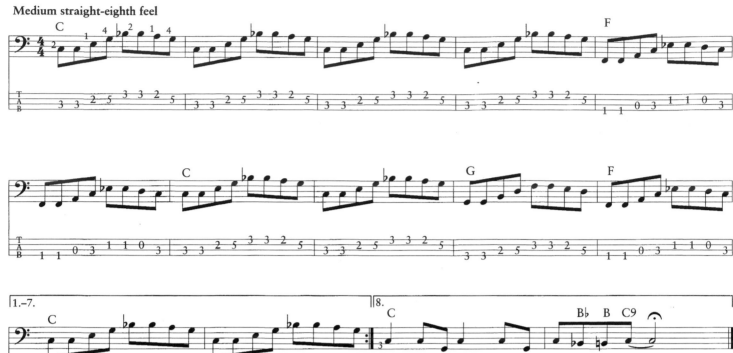

Twelve-Bar Very Slow Swing in G

We'll begin with another four-bar intro. Play this one with a nice "lazy" feel. The bassline uses both the minor third and the major third tones for each principal chord. For example, the minor third in G is B♭ while the major third is B♮. The minor third tone is often called the "blue" note.

Pattern 1: G blues scale (one-octave)

Pattern 2: C blues scale (one-octave)

Pattern 3: D blues scale (one-octave)

Twelve-Bar Very Slow Swing in G

This example will remind you of the Allman Brothers' version of the classic "Stormy Monday."

Twelve-Bar Jazzy Swing Feel in B-flat

This is still a twelve-bar blues, but as a bass player you have a lot more freedom to vary your ideas. We'll start with a four-bar intro: notice how its chord changes are the same as for the last four bars of the tune. Try accenting beats two and four a bit, and always keep the chord tones in mind.

Some arpeggios:

Below you will find laid out the arpeggios for all the chords in this tune.

dominant seventh chords

minor seventh chords

sixth chord

ninth chords

Twelve-Bar Jazzy Swing Feel in B-flat

Knockin' on the Midnight Mustang

We'll begin with a jam inspired by three classic rhythm and blues tunes: "Knock on Wood," "In the Midnight Hour," and "Mustang Sally." Each of these tunes has a killer groove, so your task is to "stay in the pocket" and be as precise about your timing as possible. Pick and choose your fills and where to put them carefully.

Patterns 1, 2, and 3: E, A, and D major triads

In this tune, as in many others, the basslines are composed mostly of chord tones. Here are three of the major triads you'll be hearing in the music.

pattern 1

pattern 2

pattern 3

Patterns 4, 5, and 6: E, A, and D major pentatonic scales

The notes that comprise the major triad also appear in each chord's respective major pentatonic scale. A major pentatonic scale is a five-note scale composed of the first, second, third, fifth, and sixth degrees of a given major scale.

pattern 4

pattern 5

pattern 6

Knockin' on the Midnight Mustang

Why a Woman Loves a Man

This next one is a nice easy slow ballad in $\frac{6}{8}$ time. For our purposes this means a triplet feel with two main beats to each bar.

Pattern 1: C major scale

This track is in the key of C major and the bassline uses the C major scale.

Why a Woman Loves a Man

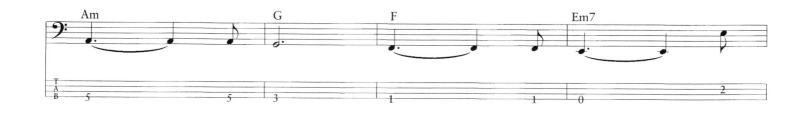

Blues Boy

This tune will remind you of Sam and Dave's "Soul Man," a tune that was made popular a second time by the Blues Brothers. The first section is the only tricky part and is based on a G major scale.

Pattern 1: G major scale

Blues Boy

Funky Blue Street

And now, here's a funk groove in the key of E. It's based on the E major pentatonic and that's it. By now we've seen enough pentatonic scales so that this should be no problem. For those of you who slap, this is a great groove to try using only your thumb. Have fun and be funky!

Pattern 1: Alternate riff pattern

Try this in place of what's written in the second and fourth bars of the C section. This line will be especially effective if you use it on the very last measure of the tune.

Funky Blue Street

Form: Intro

A 1 time
B 2 times } 3 times
C 2 times

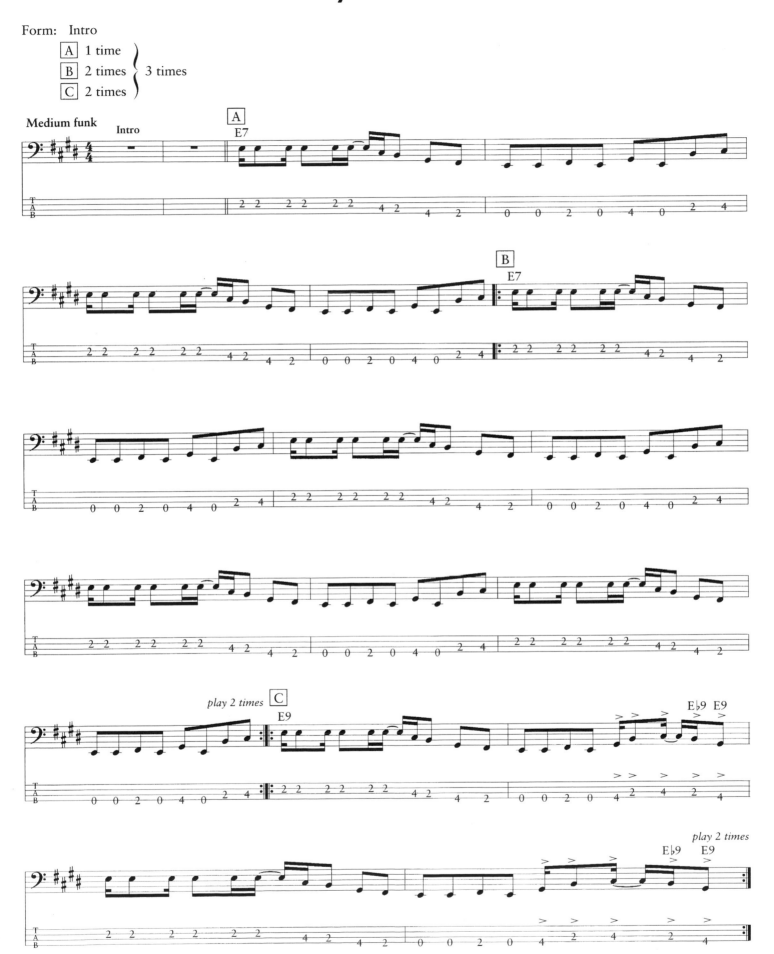

Manic Inspiration

On this particular track there is really not much room to play anything other than what is written on the chart. Keep in mind that we will be playing this one in ⅜ time with a "swing" feel. Playing with a swing feel means that consecutive eighth notes like these:

should be played like this:

Towards the end of the tune you'll be playing over a drum solo. Make sure you keep the groove together!

Notice that even though the key signature is A major, you'll be playing a lot of G♮ and C♮ notes. These come from the A minor pentatonic and A blues scales.

Pattern 1: A minor pentatonic scale with 'blue' flatted fifth note

Pattern 2: A blues scale

Manic Inspiration

The Hindenburg Medley

Okay all you Led Zeppelin fans, here it is, the ultimate Zeppelin-style jam. Once you have your parts down, you can close your eyes and pretend you're in Madison Square Garden with Jimmy Page and John Bonham.

Take note of beat four in the second bar of the D section. You can achieve this effect by "shaking" or "sliding" your fretting hand finger between the frets.

Pattern 1: Alternate C section idea

You'll find plenty of room in this section to move around; here's one of the ways you can do so.

The Hindenburg Medley

Been Caught Sleeping

Here we have a track with a nice funky groove that you can really stretch out on.
It's all steady sixteenth notes jumping around the G blues and G major scales.

Pattern 1: G blues scale

Pattern 2: G major scale

Been Caught Sleeping

Pleasantly Lucid

Last but not least, here's a ballad for all of you Pink Floyd fans. Make sure the notes ring as long as possible. This will add to the spacious and lazy feel of the track. The part we suggest is not a difficult one. Watch out for the sixteenth-note pickups and check the tablature because sometimes we'll play the same phrase but on a different part of the neck (in a different position).

Pleasantly Lucid

Now Available!

THE Jam Trax
GUITAR METHOD

Welcome to the most modern and progressive guitar method available!
All of the examples and songs included have been carefully selected in order to make
learning easy. Learn the basics of guitar playing in a way that will have you quickly jamming
with the live back-up tracks included on the CD. All examples are written in standard
notation and tablature, as well as easy-to-follow rhythmic notation.

Book 1
Basic Theory and Notation—Simple Chords and Progressions—Twelve-Bar Blues
Progression—Rhythm Studies—Basic Scale Studies—Introduction to Soloing—
and much more!

Book 2
More on Rhythm and Lead Playing—Combining Chord Shapes—More Song, Sound-Alike
Chord Progressions—Playing Tips—Live Back-Up Tracks—
and much more!

Omnibus Edition
This all-in-one volume contains the complete text, examples, and CDs of Books 1 and 2.

Also available:
JamTrax interactive book and CD packages.
Practice soloing and learn to improvise in your favorite style by jamming with the live
back-up band on the *JamTrax* CD. Learn the techniques of the professionals!
The *JamTrax* books provide suggested scales, chords, riffs, and progressions
in standard notation and tablature.

We're ready to jam when you are!

Available at your favorite music store
or call 914.469.2271 for ordering information